John Malam studied ancient history and archaeology at the University of Birmingham, after which he worked as an archaeologist at the Ironbridge Gorge Museum, Shropshire. He is now a writer, editor, and reviewer specializing in books for children. He lives in Cheshire with his wife, a book designer, and their two young children.

Dave Antram was born in Brighton in 1958. He studied at Eastbourne College of Art and then worked in advertising for 15 years before becoming a full-time artist. He has illustrated many children's non-fiction books.

Created and designed by David Salariya

Editor Karen Barker Smith

© The Salariya Book Company Ltd
MCMXCIX
All rights reserved. No part of this book may be reproduced, stored in a retrieval system or transmitted in any form or by any means, electronic, mechanical, photocopying, recording or otherwise, without the written permission of the copyright owner.

Created, designed and produced by
THE SALARIYA BOOK COMPANY LTD
25 Marlborough Place, Brighton BN1 1UB

ISBN 0 7500 2742 8

Published in 1999 by
MACDONALD YOUNG BOOKS
an imprint of Wayland Publishers Ltd
61 Western Road, Hove BN3 1JD

You can find Macdonald Young Books on the internet at http://www.myb.co.uk

A CIP catalogue record for this book is available from the British Library.

Repro by Modern Age.

Printed in Singapore

Pirates Required

Do you want to go to far-away, interesting places, meet new people, eat their food, learn their language... and get rich fast?

Adventurers are required for a trip to the Spanish Main, on board the sloop *Dolphin*, which sails out of Port Royal on the sunny island of Jamaica. You must be healthy, quick with a cutlass, good at rope-work and possess a keen eye for spotting valuables. A fine singing voice would be an asset.

Your main duties will include:

• Keeping the *Dolphin* all ship-shape and Bristol fashion – not a thing out of place and everything in good condition.

• Using axes, swords, pikes, pistols and grenades.

• Above all, you must obey the rules of the ship. Disobedient sailors will be punished.

If you think you can do this job, attend the meeting at the Singing Sailors Inn, where the crew of the *Dolphin* will be picked.

So you want to be a Pirate?

Written by
John Malam

Illustrated by
Dave Antram

MACDONALD YOUNG BOOKS

Applying for the job

The Dolphin might look small – she weighs no more than 100 tonnes and measures less than 20 metres from bow to stern – but she has a crew of 120. You have as good a chance as any of being picked.

If you can stand out from the crowd at the crew meeting, and the Captain likes what he sees, you could be off to the Spanish Main faster than you can say 'pieces of eight'.

Have a piece of rope handy so that you can demonstrate your knot-tying skills.

Show that you can take a bearing. The Captain wants seamen who can use charts and maps and can navigate.

Call out if you can read or write – the better jobs will go to those with brains, as well as brawn.

Contents

What applicants should know
5

Skills a pirate needs
6

Life on board a pirate ship
8

Captain, crew and rules of the ship
10

Clothes for the job
12

Finding your way
14

Pirate flags
16

Pirate attack!
18

Booty for all
20

Food and drink
22

A safe haven
24

Passing the time
26

Punishment and torture
28

Your interview
Glossary
30

Rogues' gallery
Index
Have you got the job?
31

What applicants should know

Be prepared for a dangerous journey – Jamaica and the other islands of the Caribbean Sea might be blessed with sun, sand and shimmering silver, but you're not going there for a holiday! You'll be taken back in time to the year 1680, and to a part of the New World where every last scoundrel, swindler, thief and drunk on Earth has fled. Port Royal, on the south coast of Jamaica is where the *Dolphin* sails from. It is a safe haven for pirates and all those who live outside the law. It has become the major city in the region with a population of about 3,000, which makes it second in size only to the English settlement of Boston, on the east coast of America. Port Royal is sheltered from storms, and on fair days sloops leave her deep harbour for the Spanish Main. This is the name given to the area that stretches from the north coast of South America to Florida in North America.

The Spanish Main, 1680

Skills a pirate needs

Have you got what it takes to be a pirate? Living on a ship doesn't suit everyone, so think hard before you decide to set your sea-legs on board the *Dolphin*. Once she's at sea there's no turning back until her hold is filled with gold, silver, and jewellery. You'll need to be tough to cope with keeping the ship in good condition, day and night. Be prepared to go without sleep until your work is done. And when a ship is attacked and taken, you'll need all the courage you can muster to protect yourself and win the fight.

Tying knots

Could you tie a knot in the dark, when you're climbing the rigging and a storm is blowing? Knots are important on board – they can join two pieces of rope together, make loops, or tie things to parts of the ship.

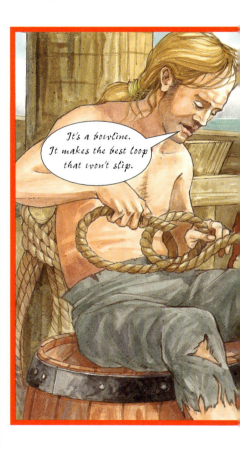

It's a bowline. It makes the best loop that won't slip.

You'll need a head for heights and a firm grip when climbing the rigging in all weathers, working on the sails, replacing ropes and pulleys, and acting as look-out.

There is never a moment to spare on board ship – one minute you could be sewing sailcloth, the next you might be busy with rope-work, tying a bowline knot at the end of a mooring rope, or using bend knots to join ropes together.

Bowline knot for making loops

art   Finish

What knot is that, lad?

Rowing and sword-fighting

When you're rowing the ship's longboat towards a prize ship, to relieve it of its valuables, you'll need strong arms and a straight back. The harder you row, the sooner you will reach your prey.

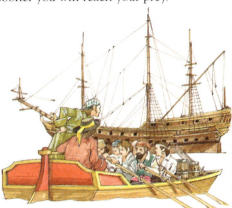

On board the prize ship you must fight with your cutlass. This is a heavy sword with a long sharp blade and a basket-shaped guard to protect your hand and wrist. Its name comes from an old French word *coutelas*, meaning 'knife'. Use it for slashing and hacking at the enemy.

Carrick bend knot   Sheet bend knot

Bend knots for joining ropes.

Life on board a pirate ship

You might be at sea for weeks before you sight a prize ship, and until then be prepared to spend hours doing routine, boring jobs. Singing songs will help pass the time. They're called shanties, (or chanties) and are half-sung, half-chanted. Often someone will make them up while he works, singing out to the others who chant back their replies. You'll lift the crew's spirits if you can whistle the tune on a pipe. Everyone has a job to do: repairing the deck, pouring molten lead to make musket balls or preparing fresh fish to eat. The point of the trip and the riches you might gain are never forgotten though – to find a ship of the Spanish treasure fleet so full of gold she's almost too heavy to sail.

Pirate sloop

Foresails

Mainsail

Caribbean pirates sail in fast ships called sloops. They have a single mast with a large mainsail and smaller foresails.

We're on our way to seek our treasure...

Only one more day together...

Treasure ship

Keep watch for a prize – a slow-sailing galleon bound for Spain with a cargo of treasure from Peru and Mexico.

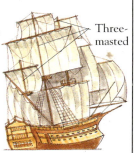

Three-masted

Keeping water out

The ship is leaking! But don't panic, all wooden ships let in water through small gaps in their hulls. It collects in the ship's bilge, from where pumps suck it up and pour it into buckets. Bilge-water stinks of rot and filth, so be careful not to spill it on deck as you empty the buckets over the side.

Bilge pump

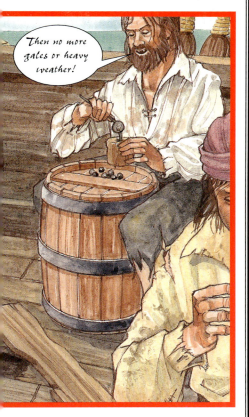

"Then no more gales or heavy weather!"

One never-ending job is caulking timbers (below). This means ramming shredded rope, called oakum, into gaps in the hull. It is then glued in place with black pitch which sets hard to make a watertight seal.

On some ships there are more rats than seamen. They gnaw their way through ropes and timbers, fill their bellies with the crew's food and spread disease. The ship's cats kill many – but if you see one, strike it hard and toss it to the sharks.

Captain, crew and the rules of the ship

The Captain expects every seaman to know his place and do his duty the best he can. In return for hard work and loyalty you will get a share of any treasure taken. The size of your share depends on the job you do. There will be no arguments about it, since you must keep to the rules you signed when you joined the ship.

Your Captain

He is the ship's commander, gives orders during battle and expects seamen to do as he says. He's been voted Captain because the crew look up to him as a strong leader.

Choosing the Captain

Before the ship sails, the crew votes which one of them should be Captain. Scuffles may break out, but after a show of hands agreement is reached on one man, who promises riches for all…

You can have my vote!

I'd rather have a rat as my Cap'n!

Cutlass

Carpenter — Surgeon — Seaman — Cabin boy — Musician

Deposing the Captain

…but if at any time he shows signs of weakness, such as refusing to go after a prize ship, or cruelty towards his men, he can be deposed. If this happens, the crew will choose another man as Captain.

Vote me Cap'n, lads, an' I'll make ye all rich!

Cook Navigator Master gunner Seamen

The Quartermaster

The Quartermaster is second-in-command and will take charge of any captured ship.

Cat-o'-nine tails

He is the only man allowed to flog (whip) a seaman. This is usually done with a cat-o'-nine tails – a whip with nine knotted lashes.

Every seaman must sign the Ship's Articles (below) and swear on the Holy Bible to obey the rules. Brawling, cheating at cards, and cowardice are forbidden and the rules also state how treasure is to be shared amongst the crew.

If you cannot write you must sign with your mark.

Clothes for the job

The clothes you stand up in are likely to be the only clothes you own. You'll work in them, fight in them and sleep in them. New clothes are expensive, and until you're lucky enough to capture the rich wardrobe of a Spaniard you can only dream about wearing the silks and satins of a gentleman. Like the other seamen on board the *Dolphin*, your clothes will be made of heavy wool, or perhaps stitched together from scraps of canvas sailcloth. You will also be barefoot. Some pirates in the Caribbean wear 'petticoat trousers' – baggy knee-length shorts which are wide at the bottom. But most make do with loose-fitting pants cut off below the knee, and a thigh-length blouse or coat.

Sailcloth for clothes

Sails are made of sailcloth which is a thick, coarse canvas woven from hemp fibres. Old pieces of sailcloth can be used to make hard-wearing clothes.

There are more holes in this sailcloth than in my shirt.

Before you board a prize ship, give your clothes a thick coating of black tar. Your enemy's sword will slip off the tar and your skin will be saved.

Keeping clean

Fresh water is for drinking, not for washing clothes and bodies. If you want to clean up, use rainwater collected in tubs. If the ship drops anchor, take a dip in the sea – but beware of sharks.

There's more filth in this bilge-water than on me.

Should you wear earrings? You might have heard stories about pirates wearing 'gypsy' hoops in their ears, made of brass or even gold. The truth is that very few pirates in the Caribbean wear any kind of jewellery – they are more interested in stealing it from their enemies. If you do wear a hoop, you might start a trend!

Rags and riches

Cocked hat with a feather
Leather belt, or baldric, for holding weapons
Velvet doublet or jacket
Silk sash
Trousers tied at the knee
Stockings
Buckled shoes

The Captain has fine clothes, stripped from the back of an enemy. Your clothes are rags of canvas, smeared in black tar to protect you from the cold and wet. You will wear them until they rot away. If you lose a leg in a fight, the carpenter will carve a wooden peg to strap to your stump.

Finding your way

The navigator uses the best scientific equipment available to find the ship's position at sea. In the daytime he takes bearings based on the height of the sun in relation to the horizon. At night, the moon and stars help him to fix the ship's course. By knowing where the ship is, the direction of her course can be worked out and plotted on charts. It is the Captain who decides where the ship sails. With the figures the navigator calculates from his measuring instruments, the Captain can check the charts to make sure the ship is sailing on the correct course.

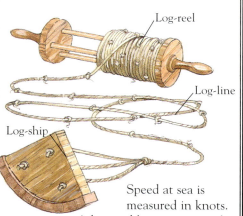

Log-reel
Log-line
Log-ship

Speed at sea is measured in knots. A knotted line is unwound over the side, and the ship is said to be sailing at so many 'knots per hour', depending on how many knots are let out in an hour.

How to use a backstaff

Stand with your back to the midday sun, hold the staff straight and look along it to the horizon. Note the angle of the shadow, from which you can work out the ship's position, called latitude.

Our course is straight and true

Land Ho!

Do not to disturb the Captain as he studies his charts. At the same time each day the navigator works out the ship's position, which the Captain plots on a chart. With his dividers he measures the distance sailed from day to day, and checks that all is well with the course.

Stock Common pattern anchor
Arm
Shank
Fluke

To bring the ship to a stop, her iron anchor is dragged along the seabed until it catches on a rock or sturdy object. Seamen say she 'rides' at anchor.

The tools of navigation

In fog you must keep watch for rocks and other dangers. The navigator will lower a lead weight to the seabed to measure the depth of water in fathoms. A fathom is the length between his arms when outstretched – 1.83 m.

Land should soon be in sight.

The navigator and Captain's instruments (below). The compass is for finding direction and the telescope enables the Captain to see land and possible prize ships from a great distance. The dividers measure distance on the charts, and by using the backstaff the navigator can calculate the ship's position.

Backstaff
Dividers
Telescope
Compass

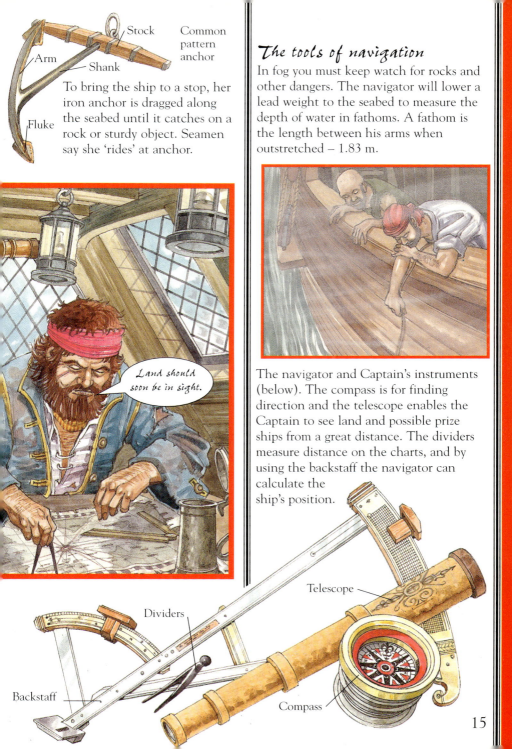

Pirate flags

Be proud of the flag the *Dolphin* flies as she engages an enemy ship – the Jolly Roger. Some believe this comes from the French *joli rouge* ('pretty red'), but others believe it originated from an Indian pirate called Ali Rajah, whose name was pronounced 'Olly Roger' by British seamen. One thing is clear, the flag's skull and crossbones are symbols understood by seamen of all nations. They stand for death and violence, and many a prize ship will surrender without a fight as soon as it spies the Jolly Roger at the top of the main mast.

If you're asked to make a Jolly Roger, the Captain will tell you what design he wants. The bolder the design, the greater the fear it will strike into your enemy's hearts.

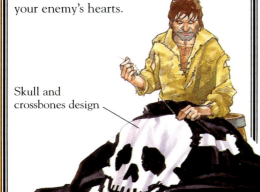

Skull and crossbones design

Raising the Jolly Roger

As in most battles, the element of surprise is the best tactic. By leaving it to the last moment to raise the Jolly Roger, your enemy will not know whether you are a friend or foe until it is too late.

Now you know who we are!

Pirate raiders are not the only bounty hunters of the Spanish Main. You will see vessels called 'privateers', which fly the flags of their countries. They are private warships which operate within the law. Their governments give them permission to plunder enemy ships so they are pirates by another name.

Your prize is in sight

As you near your prize, the enemy will see the Jolly Roger flying from the main mast. She may try to get away, but as your sloop, the *Dolphin*, is small and fast you will soon be alongside and ready to board her.

A who's who of Jolly Rogers

The skull and crossbones on a black flag. If the flag is red, all your enemy will die.

The flag of John Rackham, known as 'Calico Jack' because he wore white calico shirts.

The flag of Edward Teach, known as 'Blackbeard', who preyed on ships in the Caribbean.

The flag of Henry Every, known as 'Long Ben'. He raided ships in the Red Sea.

The two flags of Bartholomew Roberts. The letters on the top flag are the initials of men he killed. On the bottom flag a skeleton hands an hour-glass to his prey, to show that time is running out.

Flags of all nations

Britain

France

Spain

Pirate attack!

Now the prize ship knows the *Dolphin* is a pirate ship – your Jolly Roger has told them so. The next few minutes will be the most dangerous part of your work, as you board the ship and come face to face with the enemy. Some of the enemy seamen may turn against their own officers, just as keen to take the ship's riches as you are. Their mutiny will show that they have changed sides, and from now on they too are pirates. Those enemy that resist will doubtless meet a bloody end, cut down by a sword, axe or gun. During your fight call out 'No purchase, no pay!' ('no booty, no reward') and finally 'Avast!' ('stop' or 'cease').

When you're in action you must keep the match on your musket alight and your gunpowder dry. You will use a matchlock musket when shooting from a distance and a flintlock pistol for close combat. Both weapons shoot heavy balls of lead.

Pirate weapons

Light the fuse, throw it, take cover and wait for the grenade to explode, flinging lead shot in every direction.

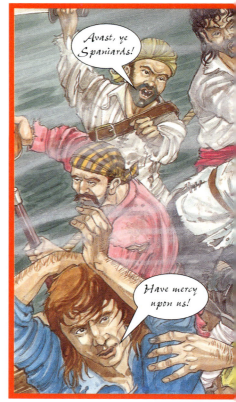

A matchlock musket (below) uses a piece of slow-burning rope (the match) to set it off.

A flintlock pistol (above) uses a flint (stone) to set it off.

Chain-shot

Chain-shot is fired into an enemy's rigging. With torn sails, a ship is dead in the water.

Cannon balls joined by chain

Firing a cannon

Sloops, like the *Dolphin*, carry small cannons which are just used to frighten the enemy – the last thing you want to do is sink the prize before you have plundered it! It takes three men to operate a cannon, firing one iron cannonball every ten minutes over a distance of about 150 m.

No purchase, no pay!

In hand-to-hand fighting use axes, swords and pikes (like spears). Keep their blades and points sharp to cut through your enemy's leather clothes.

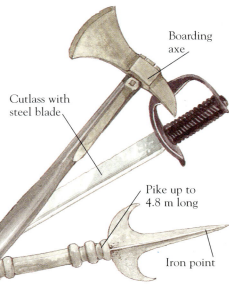

Boarding axe

Cutlass with steel blade

Pike up to 4.8 m long

Iron point

Booty for all

With an enemy ship under your control, it's time to find out what treasure she carries. Both pirates and privateers call a captured ship a 'prize', meaning 'wages' or 'reward'. The ship may contain chests of gold and silver coins, and jewellery too. The Quartermaster will take charge of whatever booty is found. He will share it amongst the seamen, according to the Ship's Articles, at the end of the voyage and not before. There are rich pickings in the Spanish Main. In 1669, Henry Morgan took 120,000 pesos (£30,000) in one raid on the Spanish treasure fleet.

Pirates look after each other. If you lose a limb, or get injured, you'll be given an extra share of the booty to make up for your loss.

Stealing provisions

Take gunpowder to refill your supplies, axes and swords that are sharper, and guns that fire better.

Fresh water and food is always welcome. It's better to be in your stomach than in your enemy's.

The Spanish were known to take gold objects from the peoples of the New World. They melted them down to make coins and these were sent back to Europe on ships.

Medicine

A medicine chest with ointments, oils, potions and doctor's tools could save your life – take it too!

The ultimate prize

The greatest prize of all may well be the enemy ship herself. Any members of her crew who do not agree to join you as pirates will be cast adrift in a longboat. The Quartermaster will take command, and the ship will sell for a good price.

You'll find no valuables on my ship.

Belay that yarn, Cap'n! (Stop your lies, Captain!)

If your prize is a galleon from the Spanish treasure fleet, her hold may be full of coins. Look for gold doubloons and silver pesos. A peso is worth eight *reales* ('royals') so pirates call them 'pieces-of-eight'.

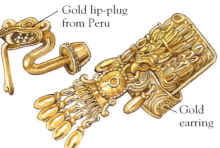

Gold lip-plug from Peru

Gold earring

Gold doubloon

Silver 'pieces-of-eight'

21

Food and drink

The *Dolphin* carries a good supply of food and drink. There should be enough to keep you fed until you take on new supplies at the next port, or at least until you seize a ship and raid its stores. Fresh food doesn't last long at sea. Even dried food, such as beans, turns bad in the damp air of the ship's hold. Only heavily salted fish and meat will last the length of the trip, and you'll soon get bored of that. Cook will do his best to hide the bad taste with spices and make strange drinks to wash your meals down. Sip 'bumboo', a mixture of rum, water, sugar, and nutmeg, and 'rumfustian', a hot drink of beer, gin, eggs, sugar, and spice.

Bottled beer
Fresh water soon turns foul on a long voyage, so the ship carries bottles of ale for the crew to drink with their food.

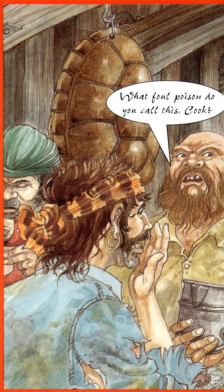

What foul poison do you call this, Cook?

A turtle is killed with a wooden club

Live sea turtles are kept on deck until needed for food. Their meat is often grilled over a smoky fire called a *barbacoa* in Spanish: the English say 'barbecue'.

If you're at sea for many weeks you will not eat many vegetables or much fresh fruit. This means you run the risk of getting scurvy – a disease caused by a lack of vitamin C. Watch out for these symptoms: blotches and sores on the skin, pimples on the gums, teeth falling out, and feeling weak.

Rum ration

You'll get a daily swig of 'kill-devil' or rumbullion, a sweet-tasting alcohol made from molasses. The English call it 'rum'.

A pirate's menu

The *Dolphin* sails with caged hens which provide fresh meat and eggs (seamen call eggs 'cackling farts'!). Fresh fish can be caught from the sea too but on days when there is no fresh food, you must chew on ship's biscuits. These are known as 'hard tack' because they're so tough. Don't complain if you find a maggot in them (they eat the biscuits too). Just close your eyes and swallow.

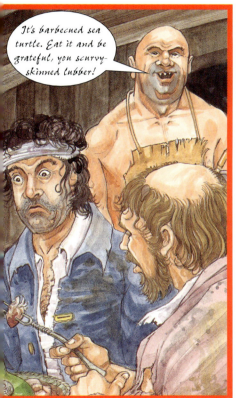

It's barbecued sea turtle. Eat it and be grateful, you scurvy-skinned lubber!

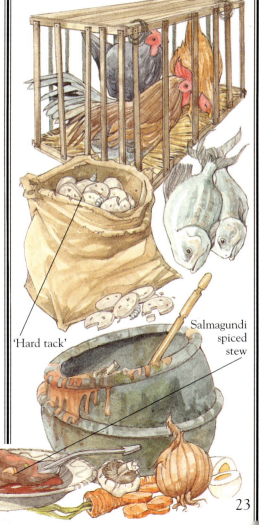

'Hard tack'

Salmagundi spiced stew

Salmagundi is a stew made from roast meat (turtle, duck, hen or pigeon), chopped into chunks and soaked in wine. Vegetables and occasionally fruit (cabbage, mangoes and onions) are thrown in and vinegar, salt, garlic, pepper and mustard are added. It's spicy!

A safe haven

Like many other pirate ships of the Spanish Main, the *Dolphin* regards the Jamaican town of Port Royal as her home port. It is a wild, lawless place which lies at the heart of the area's Spanish territories, so their treasures are within a few days sail. The town has many wealthy merchants who will buy your looted gold, silver and jewellery cheaply. They will sell it in London for a high price, and with their profits they buy supplies of food and other goods to sell to pirates in Port Royal.

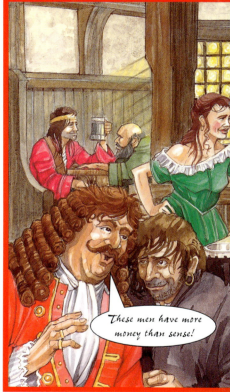

These men have more money than sense!

Enjoy life's luxuries – you'll be able to afford them now. Ask for a bottle of fine wine, but check that the cork is well tied on or else the contents could be sour.

You will be made welcome in the port's taverns, where you will find a variety of entertainment to suit the tastes of every seaman. But a word of caution. These places are the hang-outs of thieves and tricksters – both men and women – who will try to separate you from your money.

Smoking allowed

You can't smoke while you're on board ship for fear of setting it on fire – you have to make do with chewing tobacco instead. But when in port you can light up your clay pipe and smoke all day.

What to do with your riches

Some sharks live on land – the type that will cheat you out of your money at cards. They use weighted dice and a marked pack, and unless you catch them at it you'll never know you've been tricked.

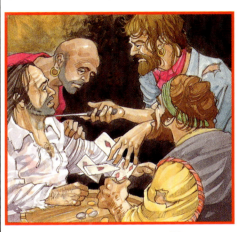

Drink and be merry!

If you bury your booty, you will tell no one where it is. Every detail will be sworn to secrecy. A map will provide the only clues.

Map

Passing the time

It's not all hard work on board the *Dolphin* – you will have some time to relax and enjoy yourself. You could practice your skills as an artist, a singer, a dancer or a musician. Or you could pluck up the courage to let a fellow seaman mark your skin with a tattoo. This new type of body art is fashionable amongst all mariners. You might even decide that this is as good a time as any to catch up on some much needed sleep. While the Captain sleeps in his private cabin, you'll sleep on the deck, or in the hold amongst the ship's ropes, barrels and other equipment. Your bed will be a hammock or a straw mattress.

Some of the men scratch pictures on to animal bones or teeth. Black soot rubbed over the marks makes them stand out. This type of art is known as 'scrimshaw', perhaps after the seaman who invented it.

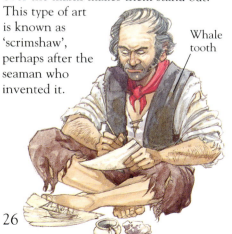

Whale tooth

Settling an argument

Be prepared to settle an argument with your bare knuckles. While you and your opponent slog it out, the rest of the ship's crew will be betting on who they think will win. Good luck to you!

Anyone for a dance? At the end of the day, when your work is done, musicians might strike up a lively tune on the fiddle and the squeeze-box. They will play a dance tune – a jig or a reel – with steps that are easy to learn. Square dances are popular, where pirates dance in pairs, or take it in turns to dance alone.

Macaws can be taught to speak

The exotic animals of the New World make excellent companions on board ship.

Monkeys can be taught tricks

"Silly old fool!"

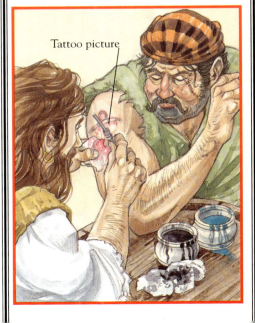

Tattoo picture

Some seamen decorate their skin with pictures by pricking it with needles. Then they rub pigments (colours) into the designs. As the skin heals, a coloured picture is left under the skin, which doesn't wash off. It became known as 'tattooing', from the Tahitian word *tattau*, meaning 'to mark'.

Punishment and torture

Hanging
Pray that you are never 'turned off the cart', an expression which means death by hanging.

As long as you are on board the *Dolphin* you are bound by the Ship's Articles and if you break the rules you will be punished. The usual form of punishment is flogging. You will be spread-eagled against a grating and the Quartermaster will whip your back with a cat-o'-nine tails. Afterwards, your back will be cut to ribbons – seamen say you have been given a 'checked shirt' to wear. Another form of punishment is keel-hauling, where the unfortunate seaman is dragged under water from one side of the ship to the other. If he survives, the half-drowned man may well die from the cuts he got as his body was pulled over the razor sharp barnacles which grow on the ship's hull.

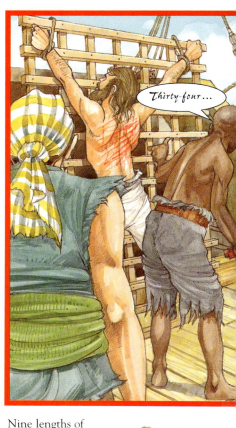

The cat-o'-nine tails is made by the man to be flogged, as part of his punishment.

Nine lengths of knotted rope

Torture

If you are caught as a pirate you may be tortured. Will you take the pain, or will you tell them where your booty is?

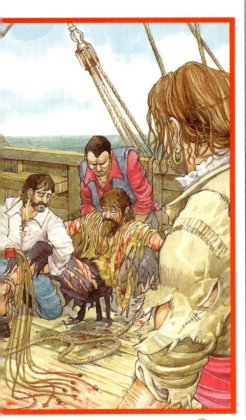

The body of an executed pirate swings from a gibbet. It is clamped inside a metal cage so it will still look human as it rots. The grisly remains are placed at the water's edge to act as a warning to others who may be tempted into a life of piracy.

Gibbet

Your ship sails away

If you are marooned you will be left on a remote island by yourself. When the supplies the crew gave you runs out you will have to look for food.

29

Your interview

Answer these questions to test your knowledge, then look at the opposite page to find out if you have got the job.

Q1 What are musket balls made of?
A   Gold.
B   Silver.
C   Lead.

Q2 What is a bowline?
A   A knot.
B   A weapon.
C   A dance.

Q3 How do you use tobacco on ship?
A   Smoke it.
B   Chew it.
C   Sniff it.

Q4 What type of songs will you sing?
A   Shanties.
B   Jigs.
C   Reels.

Q5 What is salmagundi?
A   Spiced beer.
B   Spiced stew.
C   Spiced fruit.

Q6 What do you do with a 'cackling fart'?
A   Fire it from your pistol.
B   Stamp on it before it bites.
C   Eat it.

Q7 What is keel-hauling?
A   Being dragged around the deck.
B   Being dragged under water.
C   Being dragged to the top of the mast.

Q8 Who is second in command?
A   The Quartermaster.
B   The navigator.
C   You.

Glossary

Backstaff A tool for working out the position of a ship.

Bilge The lowest compartment of a ship.

Booty Stolen goods.

Bow The front of a ship.

Cat-o'-nine tails A whip used for flogging.

Cutlass A pirate's sword.

Doubloon Spanish gold coin.

Galleon A large merchant ship.

Hold The area used for stores and sleeping quarters under the deck.

Knot A unit of measurement for a ship's speed.

Lip-plug An ornament worn in a hole cut through the lower lip.

Marooned To be abandoned.

Mutiny When the crew overrule the Captain and take control of their ship.

New World North and South America in relation to Europe.

Piece-of-eight The nickname for a Spanish eight *reales* silver coin.

Pitch A black, resin-like liquid.

Privateer A type of pirate ship whose crew works for a government.

Prize Ship A ship taken as wages or a reward.

Sailcloth Tough canvas for sails. Also used for making hard-wearing clothes.

Shot Small lead pellets used in shotguns.

Sloop A small, fast sailing ship.

Stern The back of a ship.

Tar A thick black liquid made from coal. Also a slang name for a sailor.

Tattoo A picture drawn into the skin which is then permanent.

Rogues' gallery

Wild women

Anne Bonny
She became a pirate on John Rackham's ship but had to dress as a man to hide her identity, as women were not allowed on pirate ships. In 1720, Rackham's ship was seized during raids along the north coast of Jamaica. On board were Bonny, Mary Read, Rackham and eight other men. The men were hanged, but Bonny and Read were spared because they were pregnant.

Grace O'Malley
An Irish female pirate who raided ships along the west coast of Ireland between 1560 and 1580. Even though she was caught, Queen Elizabeth I pardoned her.

Mary Read
An English pirate who fought alongside Anne Bonny on board John Rackham's ship.

Mean men

Henry Every
English pirate of the 1690s who raided ships in the Red Sea but died penniless in England.

William Kidd
Scottish-American pirate of the 1690s. He turned to piracy after working as a privateer and was eventually hanged.

Sir Henry Morgan
Welsh pirate who raided cities in Central America and the Caribbean in the 1660s.

John Rackham
English pirate who was hanged in 1720.

Bartholomew Roberts
Successful Welsh pirate who was killed during an attack in 1722.

Edward Teach
English pirate feared for his appearance, hence his nickname 'Blackbeard'. Fought with fuses burning in his hair. Died in battle in 1718.

Index

Page numbers in bold refer to illustrations

B
booty 18, **20**, **25**, 29, 30

C
Captain 4, **10-11**, 13, 14, **15-16**, 26, 30
clothes **12-13**, 17, 19, 30
crew 2, 4, **8**, **10-11**, 21, **29**, 30
cutlass 2, **7**, **10**, **19**, 30

E
enemies **7**, 13, **16-17**, **18-19**, 20, **21**
entertainment **24-25**, **26-27**

F
fighting **6-7**, **12-13**, **18-19**, 26, **27**
food 2, **8**, 9, 20, **22-23**, 24, 29

J
Jolly Roger 4, **16-17**, 18

N
navigation 2, 4, **14-15**

P
pieces-of-eight 4, **21**, 30

Have you got the job?

Count up your correct answers and find out if you got the job.

8 (A) page 11
7 (B) page 28
6 (C) page 23
5 (B) page 23
4 (A) page 8
3 (B) page 25
2 (A) page 6
1 (C) page 18

pirates
Blackbeard 17, 31
Bonny, Anne 31
Every, Henry 17, 30
Kidd, William 31
Morgan, Henry 20, 31
O'Malley, Grace 31
Rackham, John 17, 31
Read, Mary 31
Roberts, Bartholomew 17, 31
privateers 16, 20, 30, 31
prize ships **7**, **8-9**, 11, 12, 15, **16-17**, **18-19**, **20-21**, 30
punishment **28-29**, 31

Q
Quartermaster 11, 20-21, **28**

R
rope 2, 4, **6-7**, 9, 18, 26, **28**, 30

S
Ship's Articles 11, 20, 28
Spanish Main 2, **4-5**, 16, 20, 24

T
treasure 8-9, 10-11, **20-21**, **24-25**

W
weapons 2, **7**, 8, **10-11**, **18-19**, 20, 30
women **24**, 31

Your score:
8 Congratulations: a pirate's life is obviously the one for you.
7 Not quite ready: but if someone drops out before the *Dolphin* leaves port, you can join us.
5-6 Promising: you have the qualities – try again when we're back in port.
3-4 Not ready yet: your sea-legs are too shaky.
Below 3 Too bad: you're only fit for fishfood.

31

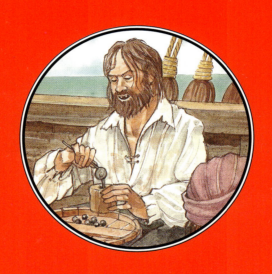

A GHOST IN LOVE
AND OTHER PLAYS

Stage 1

Most people do not believe in ghosts, until they see one with their own eyes. In these three plays, Richard, Jenny and Brad all have their lives changed completely by the ghosts who appear to them.

Richard Little is surprised and very afraid when he sees the ghost of his dead brother-in-law. He knows that he must help the ghost to find peace, although he himself will be in great danger.

When Jenny Lawson meets the ghost of her dead husband, she understands that he has a special message for her – something that he did not manage to tell her when he was alive.

And finally, in the title play, Brad Davis meets the ghost of the girl he loved and left three hundred years ago. Is he going to stay with her and make her happy, or return to twentieth-century America?

Michael Dean, the author of these plays, is a writer who lives and works in Colchester, in the south-east of England.

OXFORD BOOKWORMS PLAYSCRIPTS
Series Editor: Clare West

OXFORD BOOKWORMS

For a full list of titles in all the Oxford Bookworms series,
please refer to the *Oxford English* catalogue.

OXFORD BOOKWORMS PLAYSCRIPTS

Stage 1

The Murder of Mary Jones *Tim Vicary*
A Ghost in Love and Other Plays *Michael Dean*
Sherlock Holmes: Two Plays *Sir Arthur
Conan Doyle (retold by John Escott)*

Stage 2

Romeo & Juliet *William Shakespeare
(retold by Alistair McCallum)*